SUBS

MW00881614

David Allport

I'd like to dedicate this book to every substitute teacher. We do much more than, "fill in a time slot when a teacher is out." We can and do make a difference in our schools and in the lives of each precious student."

SUBSTITUTE TEACHING 101

INTRODUCTION

Special thanks to Cecile Esposito, Pete Gardner, and Andy Zack. They have been a real help in this project.

INTRODUCTION

No matter where I go online, I still haven't been able to find a university or college offering a major or minor in subbing nor even a course or class that offers training for substitute teachers.

Oh, each county, state or third party provider of substitute teachers will have a manual, but a lot of those are just like reading from a dictionary!

I've learned over the years that people's attention is best held through stories. Thus I have incorporated many of those in this book.

Also you'll find a lot of practical principles in this that are not necessarily politically correct or something you'd read from a manual. These are practices that I have put into use with a lot of success.

I'm now in my 15th year of subbing. I'm semi-retired and do not have any inkling of retiring any time soon. By the way, I've been learning the new definition of, "retirement." ….FOUR NEW TIRES AND REFIRE! LOL

My email and contact information is at the end of this book. If you have any questions or if I can be of any help to you please do not hesitate to contact me.

1- I AM LISTENING

"But Mr. A, why can't we just talk?" The student with the curly hair and green football jersey gave the new substitute teacher a half smile with a pleading look.

"Tell you what," the fourth grade sub with the trimmed silver beard exclaimed with a warm smile. "I'll offer this class a deal concerning talking."

By now the attention of the whole class had been obtained, and all eyes were on the tall blue eyed sub. There was true quiet in Ms. Brown's elementary classroom, now being led by Mr. A, a seasoned substitute teacher, having credentials to sub in three counties, along with his credentials to teach in the state.

"I'll get to disclosing this deal in a little bit, but first let me show you what the three things you should do when I call your name during attendance.

He continued, "But there is one thing that we need to establish before we get to those three things. How many of you think talking or listening is more important?

Raise your left hand if you think talking is more important?"

Of the 22 students in the class 3 hands went up and not all of those responses were done with the left hand.

"Ok, raise your right hand if you think listening is more important than talking."

At this juncture a lot of right hands shot up into the air. As all the students looked around the room, it was clear that the majority had chimed in, and that the acknowledgement was written on the young faces of the 9 and 10 year olds in the room that listening was indeed preeminent over talking.

One young man in the front row raised his hand, but did not wait for Mr. A to give the go ahead to talk, he blurted out, "Listening is more important!"

Mr. A ignored the lack of proper protocol this time and responded, "And why is that young man?"

"Cuz it just is!" declared the boy.

"Is that so? Ok, does anyone else have an opinion?"

Mr. A scanned the room and waited.

A hand went up in the air and a girl with long brown hair and bright brown eyes waited for the sub to nod and give her the go ahead to talk.

"Because I learn better when I'm listening." She said it loud enough and with just the right force, that her words had an air of certainty about them.

"Excellent response young lady," Mr. A continued, "Another great reason for listening over talking is that God gave each of us two ears and one mouth, could it be that simple math tells us we should spend twice as much time listening than talking?"

At this idea the class got real quiet and it was obvious that the wheels were turning in their gray matter.

One of Mr. A's ongoing goals in teaching was to encourage his students to learn to think for themselves.

On this day he was subbing in the county next to the county that had adopted the motto, "I AM LISTENING."

This saying was plastered all over the place in the various K-12 schools, via posters, placards, signs and even in beautifully stenciled glossy banners that must have cost the school system a pretty penny.

Another hand was raised in the classroom and this student waited for Mr. A to give him the floor, "So what's the deal about what you mentioned earlier?"

Mr. A smiled at the whole class and said,"If you work hard and do not talk for 30 minutes, I will let you have the last 20 minutes of class to work with a partner."

At this the class seemed to express their approval in a unified rhythm at the sub's preconceived bargain.

From that point on the class was smooth sailing, and had shown that the motto, " I AM LISTENING," had indeed penetrated their minds and hearts. Mr. A was happy because now he could get back to his current library book, a real page turner entitled, PORTRAITS of COURAGE by George W. Bush.

SUMMARY:
1- Bring your classes To realize listening is the key to learning.
2- Use class protocol and listening exercises to drive home the preeminence of listening for learning.

2- ORDER OR DISORDER

"Preparation is the separation between winning and losing"

As a substitute teacher, just walking into an assigned classroom can be more than a hint about the rest of the day, by just looking at the overall condition of the room.

First impressions are important.

Good days are usually ones where I enter the classroom and all is clean. Pencils on the floor, papers scattered, and a scribbled marker board, are not a good sign.

The teacher's desk is usually the prime place to look to see if the day will be smooth sailing or a rough day at sea. It's always a delight to see a desk which simply has on it all the papers and various implements needed for that day.

One day I walked into a high school culinary class. It was immaculate. The handouts were labeled as to which pile went to which class.

When I took attendance the seating charts were accurate. The emergency instructions were neatly placed in a folder in good order. (Fire drill, live shooter, bomb threat. Etc.)

Before class starts, I make sure that I have everything laid out in order, the main items being:

1- The lesson plans of the teacher.
2- Class roster for every period.
3- The bell schedule for when classes change.
4- A handwritten chart with a circle for every desk as it's laid out in the classroom. Ready to put the student's name in the circle for their desk when I do attendance.

I always leave teachers detailed notes so they can get a bit of a grasp of how the day went when they were absent. Some teachers will leave their cell number in case you, as the sub, have a question or something comes up that you need advice about right then.

It's always nice to be able to write to the regular teacher to say thank you for the well-written instructions.

There are other days when I feel I can't leave a note like that. Why? The disorder of the teacher's desk and or instructions. Thankfully this does not happen much.

Have you ever noticed that you can look in a person's car and usually tell if they have order or disorder in their life?

In the schools I work in, I use the teacher's desk to determine that instructor's order or lack thereof.

Recently I subbed in a middle school and the first thing I noticed was that there were piles of disheveled miscellaneous papers in random areas of this teacher's desk. The instructions for the day were nowhere to be found, no bell schedule when classes were to switch, and just barely enough room on the desk to put the attendance sheet. No emergency instructions, etc. You get the picture in other words…

A ROYAL MESS!!

I found that a lack of organization translates to more work for me, chasing down other teachers to find out what to do, or just trying to find out what is needed in the chaotic array of disorder is always a major task.

On the bright side after many years of subbing, I have found that most teachers have order, and do not leave the desk like a tornado hit it.

 Let me say that as a substitute teacher you really learn to respect all teachers. For many many reasons they are so important to the future sanity, education and prosperity of our society in America.

SUMMARY:
1- Documentation of the day's events is essential for the review of the teacher I am subbing for.
2- Preparation is a key to success.

3- SUBSTITUTE TEACHER AN OXYMORON?

"Like summer snow YOU were an unexpected sight…"
Keith Green

"What do you mean you don't do anything when you sub Harry?"

"I mean just that! This is the easiest job I have ever had." Harry snickered at his friend Stu, who was trying to light a big cigar he'd just got from a pal who had just got back from Havana, Cuba on vacation.

"Yeah I just heard from Julie that it is a breeze, but she says it depends on which grade you are teaching." Stu was now puffing his huge Cuban handmade stogie as the two close friends were enjoying the aftermath of a great dinner at their favorite downtown grill.

"Yep she's got that right, I quit doing K-2 months ago, too much work, the kids haven't yet learned what the word, "no," means. Also about the only middle school job I like is gym class. Middle school can have a lot of attitude on steroids, drama and maintenance.

Harry swatted a mosquito that was trying to draw blood from his forearm.

"Hey man I heard you all got a raise after the virus. You are up to $15, $16 an hour if you have a bachelor's degree! That's pretty good pay for not really doing anything, and sitting on your duff.

What do you mean Stu?

Well isn't it the truth that the words substitute teacher is an oxymoron?

Stu actually had his buddy put his Michelob Ultra on the table, mouth wide open at that quip, having stretched his long tired legs at the outdoor patio of the Irish Pub they were at. Harry was a bit dumbfounded. First, that his buddy would use such a big word, and second he himself had forgotten what the word meant.

"OK wise guy, an oxymoron?"

Stu decided not to quiz his friend on the word's meaning, "two words that don't belong together like summer snow or immense ant.

"Oh," Harry mused.

"Julie told me besides taking attendance when subbing at high school and writing, "Google Classroom," for the lesson plans on the board all you do is sit on your big behind, amigo!"

"Well I have to admit she is spot on when it comes to nailing down that job description." Harry took another swig of his cold brew, "By the way Romeo when you are going to get around to asking Julie out?

"Soon, Mr. Sub.' Stu was in fact going to call Julie that night and ask her if she wanted to go out for dinner Saturday night. Stu took another long draw on his cigar, and flicked the ashes, "So I am really interested how'd you say that I could get hired for subbing?"

"I'll give you the website address." Harry pulled out his phone and sent the address via texting to Stu's phone.

Harry grinned and said,"It's your turn to pick up the tab for dinner, and thanks for recommending the Shepherd's Pie…. Outstanding!"

"Alright Harry, I got this," Stu flipped his debit card on the tab tray. "Remember you mentioned you would give me a crash course on subbing, if I decided to take the plunge, well I'm ready to dive in! You gotta mentor me man on how to become an effective sub, so plan on giving me that lecture soon, Mr. Substitute Teacher!"

"Here's your first lesson Stu, my real title should not be Substitute Teacher but Substitute Order Keeper!"

SUMMARY:
1- Substitute teaching is usually more about maintaining order in the class, then actually teaching the students.

4- TAKING ATTENDANCE AND CLASS PROTOCOL

"Greet the friends by name."
3 John 14

"Dylan Conway!"

I heard somebody say, "Here," but I didn't see a hand go up in the air. With so many kids in the class, it's really hard to know who said it, if many of them are talking. As they were coming in before the pledge of allegiance there were many voices talking at the same time.

"If you could please remember to raise your hand when you say, "Here,"; this will go a lot quicker, and then we will have more time to do other things in class." I used a volume with my voice where all of the students were alerted that it was time to stop talking and pay attention.

I always remind myself to say please and thank you when I'm interacting with the students. This is really important because they will replicate and mirror the behavior of the teacher.

"Dylan Conway, OK Dylan, I see your hand now, thank you."

Before school starts I draw the class room by desks, I use circles for desks because it takes less time. This hand written rooming chart, I then use the chart for various things as the class develops. Besides their names, I write down on this chart behaviors that are not appropriate or students that were helpful, the time a student leaves for the bathroom and then the time they return, which student took attendance to the office, to name a few uses of the chart. This is information the teacher will be glad to access the next day.

The pledge of allegiance and the moment of silence was next. Thankfully this was a school that didn't just have a hiccup or like 2 seconds for the moment of silence over the loudspeaker and there was really time to pray during the moment of silence. I pray each time, I will do my work unto the Lord with a spirit of excellence.

Before I address the need for order and talking, it is important that all the creatures in the room must be immobilized by being seated.

Here you can get your first taste of the obstinate and those who are the attention seekers.

"Would everyone please be seated!"

I also remember to smile.

First impressions are important and these children don't know me, and I don't know them, but I want them to know that I am a friendly substitute teacher, and that I smile often.

I usually stand in the front of the class to take attendance but sometimes I sit at the teacher's desk and draw the handwritten rooming chart accordingly.

Sometimes a little extra volume is needed when students are just being seated, and getting oriented to being in class.

The first few minutes are preeminent in order for you to establish ongoing order.

Taking attendance is an art and can be an adventure. Middle School classes are not my favorite animal to tame, yet with this particular age group, if you do not proactively tame this species, they will soon take control of the classroom that you are supposed to be in charge of.

High school can be challenging too; it just depends on the class and the school that you're in.

By the way, one of my mottos in subbing is, "Control the class without being controlling."

So just what are you talking about? And just what is really important in the beginning and throughout the class time?

"PROTOCOL."

High schoolers and a lot of the Middle School classes do not require as intricate an amount of protocol as I use in elementary school. With high school I simply take attendance, and then turn them loose to whatever the teacher has assigned them to do.

The following is the protocol that I use when I'm in elementary school.

Once all are seated then I turn to the board where I have three things listed:

1- Raise your hand if you want to talk.
2- Say please if you want something like going to the bathroom.
3- Remember to say,"thank you."

Number one- One person talks at a time.

Number two- You may not talk in class unless you raise your hand and receive permission from me to talk, here you can point to the board again to reiterate what you've already communicated.

Number three- Even if you raise your hand I might not call on you right away the translation of this is, you may have to wait to speak.

Number four- If you want to go to the bathroom, (by the way that is the only place I am authorized to send you), so please do not ask to go elsewhere. Thank you.

Number five- Please and thank you are the three most important words in this classroom.

Side note: I do not let students go to the bathroom unless they say please.

So today it was 9/11 otherwise known as Patriots Day, and one of the students last name was Kennedy.

"Is there anyone in this class that knows what took place on September 11, 2001?"

Not one hand went up in the air.

"Okay does anybody know the story about what happened in New York City when the Twin Towers were bombed?"

A girl in the second row raised her hand.

I looked at my rooming list and responded.

"Ok Jenna what happened?"

"Didn't two airplanes crash into those towers and start big fires?"

"That's correct, how did you know that?"

"My dad was NYPD, and helped with the rescue."

This led me to an idea for a story later in the class. I waited till the end of class and told the story of knowing where I was at 9/11 and during the assassination of JFK.

Something most Americans can recall if they were alive then.

I need all the help I can get, and I have found prayer is an effective way to get help in time of need.

Eye contact is essential.

In communication with classes, long ago, I learned the importance of what's called spotting and scanning.

Scanning involves looking every single person in the eye as you scan around the room while you are communicating.

Spotting is when you focus on one individual, and the feeling in the class by doing this is students think you're talking just to them. It's very effective.

So now it is time to take attendance.

I make sure it is quiet and I have their undivided attention, I see if they are willing to give me their attention:

"When I say your name I need you to do three things."

Number one- Raise your hand
Number two- Look at me
Number three- Say here with a big voice
Number four- I say is optional and that would be to smile.

Then I start calling names checking them either here or absent also I begin to start my handwritten rooming chart more on this later.

Names have changed since I was a kid. Names were Susan,Tom, Ronnie, Jim, Nancy, Cindy, Mike and Ann, Ann was my girlfriend in kindergarten. I used to walk her home, but now in my hometown children aren't allowed to do that, because of the very real threat of child abduction and kidnapping.

As I am beginning to call out their names, I asked them to correct me if I mispronounce anyone's name.

Trust me they do!

Dale Carnegie, the 20th century tycoon, philanthropist and author of, "How to Win Friends and Influence People," in the book, one of the chapters is entitled "The sweetest sound to any human being is the sound of their own name."

Names are important.

Therefore I always seek to say the name accurately, by the way I mess it up on a regular basis and mispronounce... LOL

Names nowadays are Rhiannon Jaden, Jose, Qi'Shaun, Aiden, Talayah, Mykaylla, Aaliyah, Earmie, TyQuan,and Emma, you see what I mean. Thus it would seem parents now want unique names for their children.

I do the best I can to pronounce them phonetically and accurately.

You ask why such a fuss about something as simple as taking attendance? Funny you should ask, let me tell you why in outline form:

1- As I say each name I make eye contact and try to read the individual's attitude.

2- As I hear them say,"here," much is revealed.
Was it a mousy voice?
Was it loud?
Did they even say here?

If they did not or I did not hear them I will ask nicely did you say,"here?"

A response or non-response can also be a great telltale of their personal behavior and a hint to the future with them in this classroom.

As I go through the names, if they are here, I check them off. If not I write an Ab for absent. Once finished I try to pick someone who looks responsible to take the sheet down to the office.

 The students that are rebellious, contrarians, over the top talkers, naysayers, complainers, critics, and cynics can usually be spotted in this process which usually does not eat up a lot of time.

Another helpful thing I do is using the pause and stare technique with the misbehaving child.

If it's multiple talkers then I out talk them and keep talking, many times focusing my eyes on the children who are talking when they should not be, until they are all quiet I say things like:

" I need it quiet," and put one finger up.
Then if that doesn't work I say,
" I need it quiet." and put up two fingers in the air, trying to make eye contact with everybody if it goes to number three that class is in hot water.

Another technique I say is," may I have your attention please. I'm waiting for all to be quiet." Staring at the talkers, sometimes I put an index finger on my mouth, to clearly communicate that quietness is not a suggestion, but rather a command.

Let me close this chapter by saying how important it is to smile. It's an easy act and behavior for one to forget.

When people don't know you, smiling is essentially, very very important, it's like the poster of the teacher that I'm subbing for today says,

TALK LESS SMILE MORE

SUMMARY:
1- Wisdom in substitute teaching involves calling the students by name.
2- Take the time and effort to make a hand written rooming chart while doing attendance.
3- Teaching children to be polite, this becomes a bonus you impart to them.

5- SPEAKING IN THE THIRD PERSON IS AN EFFECTIVE ROD

"Spare the rod and spoil the child"

"Aiden, you and Emma come here," the smirk that was on his face disappeared, and Emma's facial expression all of a sudden went from happy-go-lucky to troubled and worried.

Right then you could hear a pin drop in the room. Every eye was on the two that were being called up to the teacher's desk for excessive talking, they slowly marched up to the front of the room. They had already been warned along with all the other students in the classroom that they needed to be quiet, so work could be done more effectively.

As they approached my desk I signaled for them to walk behind the desk where I was, so they could look at my seating chart that I had made by hand.

As their eyes lit on my handwritten rooming list chart, I pointed to the picture of the two desks where they were seated in the room with their names written on the circles that I had made for desks. I said in a quiet whisper so no one else in the class could hear. "Do you see these two students?" Then I make sure that they realize I'm talking about them, "I thought I just saw these two talking, is that right?"

At this point Emma blurted out, "I was only trying to help him with his work!" Then I said, "Were you two talking, yes or no?

They both said yes and then I whispered, thank you for choosing to be honest. I did not call you up here to embarrass you but to correct you.

I have good news and bad news for you. The bad news is you were talking and I have to put a check mark by your name.

The good news is I believe in mercy, and giving students a second chance when they do not follow directions. So if I do not hear another peep out of you two, I will cross out that check mark at the end of the day, and your teacher will not know anything about this, but if I find you talking again your teacher will know and I will write you up.

I never heard another word out of either one of them, for the rest of the class.

Also the rest of the class got working and stopped talking.

Why?

Because they knew they would be next if caught talking.

Occasionally I have a student or two who do not want to be in the class.

What do you mean?

I mean if they continue to disrupt and talk that tells me they do not want to stay. I'm clear that if I have to call the office, it is because their actions are in effect saying they do not want to stay.

I tell them I don't want anyone to get in trouble. I don't like writing people up, and certainly don't want anyone to leave, but they can choose to leave by chronic bad behavior.

Yesterday in class a young man fell asleep in the first period. I proceeded to gently wake him up and gave him a blank sheet of paper so he could join the class in doing the assignment. The assignment was to write a paragraph about the person they chose to listen to from a collection of people on their laptop with headphones, who had experienced the World Trade Towers debacle, in New York City on September 11, 2001.

10 minutes later his head was buried in his computer fast asleep again. He forced me to call the office at extension 5600 and to that Middle School's credit two administrators were there in less than a minute and a half.

When these administrators showed up I said, "Sorry to bother you, but this young man would not stay awake. I woke him up 10 minutes ago, and gave him a paper, and encouraged him to do his work, but he fell asleep again. He needs to go somewhere else.

This young man made some sort of distasteful grunt as he got up and was walking out with a frown.

Then I looked at the rest of the class and calmly said, "Is there anyone else that needs to go out now, I don't want to have to bother these gentlemen again."

At that point each student was riveted to their chair and did not make a sound or move.

Here are a couple of helpful notes for you:

1- Corporal punishment was for the most part done away with in the 1960s, there are however some schools that will exercise it, if the parents give written permission to the front office.

2- I refer to the rod as being a neutral object not a person's hand, in this case the hand written rooming list is a neutral object along with the phone.

3- The volume of your voice is important. I have found that when I lower my voice it can be many times more effective than when I raise it, but yes I will raise it when I need to.

4- Eye contact is huge. If you can be easily embarrassed, substitute teaching is not for you. Students will stare at you to see if you are timid or fearful… be ready because they will be ready for you, to take advantage of you if possible.

SUMMARY:
1- Correction with a neutral object is a good choice.
2- Correction to correct and not to embarrass is the right path.

6- THE OLD WEST AND THE APP THAT ALERTS FOR SUB JOBS

"Festus, Get over here and help Doc with his patient" Matt Dillon

I truly love a good Western! John Wayne, Audey Murphy, Clint Eastwood, Robert DuVall, and Kevin Costner…. These men really knew how to do a Western. Mr. Costner is still doing them.

The look, the clothes, the saloon, the horses, the boots,the smell of leather, gun smoke, the cattle, the prairie, the guns, the rifles, and of course the great stories could always carve out a book or movie that was thrilling, nail biting, sensitive and impressive. This with the right author like my favorite Louis L'Amour, is a recipe for greatness.

For this chapter I want to focus on one big element of Western life. It was a way many men chose to settle their differences. This was how justice was administered at times, unfortunately, and yet was quick and decisive.

It was called, "the drop."

It was when someone was able to get a gun pointed at you faster than you could get one pointed at them.

Sometimes a draw was involved, like a gunfight in the middle of the street.

It could mean someone sneaking up on you from behind.

However it came about, "the drop," was always final.

You ask what does this have to do with substitute teaching?

Good Question.

First of all, the days of a phone call to get an assignment are virtually over. Jobs are normally secured online. Although one of the counties that I am certified in to sub still uses this outdated method, that being the telephone.

This phone app does not have much to do with the classroom activity itself, but how you get into the classroom via when you are alerted of a job. Then in turn you either accept or reject the job by pushing the appropriate button/tab on your phone or computer.

There are a number of apps designed to alert you when a job becomes available, usually by text message notification sound

The ones I have used are relatively inexpensive.

They can be a great resource and helpful to gain new job assignments.

Here's the snag.

My alert sounds and I think to myself, "Yeah I got a high school job!" Only to find out when I push the button to accept, my app tells me, "job is no longer available."

Darn it!

Someone got, "the drop," on me.

I'm finding a lot of subs are quicker than I am on, "the drop."

So now you know the parallel between the Old West and how subbing jobs are obtained.

Thankfully there are usually still enough jobs to go around.

SUMMARY:

1- Attention to the app alert notification sound on your smartphone can and will make the difference of you getting a job or not.

7- HEY GOOGLE! TEACHING STUDENTS TO THINK

"So how many of you think most books come from movies?" A few hands went up in the English class. "All right, how many of you think that most movies come from books?" Over half the class raised their hands on this.

"Okay so more of you believe that movies come from books rather than the other way around right?" The teacher always tried hard to make eye contact with every student.

"So why do the majority of you believe that? Who can try and answer for the class?"

The teacher called on a student about three rows back.

"Well it just makes sense to me. I'd rather read a book than watch a movie any day."

"Why's that?"

The student thought about that for quite a while and responded.

"Because with a book I get to take my time and use my imagination. With a movie the producers don't leave any room for that because they're showing you on the screen what they think it should look like."

Later that day when the teacher was reflecting on that student's answer, he saw that that young man was truly starting to learn how to think for himself.

Unfortunately for a lot of young Americans who have cut their teeth on learning by going to a search engine and asking questions, they may be learning a lot of facts about things, but not necessarily going through the thought process for themselves of how to obtain wisdom.

I've heard it said that knowledge is having facts, but wisdom is knowing what to do with them.

As a substitute teacher we don't necessarily have a lot of time with the same students, but the time that we do have we can help these students to learn to think for themselves.

How?

First of all by asking them questions that make them think, *just how am I going to come up with the answers*. As we know in the real world things are not always cut and dried and black and white.

Teaching students to explore their feelings by asking questions can be very beneficial.

Showing students how to think inductively.

By asking themselves these questions:
1- Who is saying this?
2- What does this mean?
3- Where is this taking place?
4- When are the events taking place?
5- How are things happening?
6- Why is this or that going on?

If all we are doing is telling students the answers and having them fill in the blanks, then are they really learning how to think for themselves?

Another important aspect of learning to think for oneself is to teach students that failure is not final, but often a stepping stone to learning how to do things better.

It is the wise substitute teacher that utilizes their time well to help students truly learn to think for themselves.

The leaders of high-tech corporations very wisely created systems that made it easier for teachers and students to communicate, and even to do their work on those companies' platforms. One such company is Google which of course invented the Google Classroom app which is used in most schools in the United States.

Another corporation early on gave schools huge discounts on their computers, and that would be Apple. Students were then learning to use their system so of course when they got out of school they weren't looking to buy Hewlett-Packard, Dell or one of the other competitors. They became loyal to the systems they were learning on in school.

Microsoft made software easier to use with Windows.

I see that one of the largest challenges in this day and age is to show and demonstrate to students that their intelligence, and the brain that they've been given, will always be more valuable and powerful than anything man can come up with online, in cyberspace, AI or using algorithms.

Please don't get me wrong. I believe these tools are very useful, and we live in a day and age when the nano world is just fascinating, and can be very helpful. As the most read book of all time has said about this era, "knowledge has increased, and people are going to and fro."

But nothing compares with what has always been, and that is a good well-prepared teacher showing a student how important it is to think for themselves.

SUMMARY:

1- Self government can be lost in our cyber world easily. Make a serious effort to help students think about what they are doing. Then they will learn to make good choices based on their own thought process and not AI or a search engine.

8- OMITTING CURSIVE & SCRIBBLE DIBBLE

The other day I was calling up individuals to check their work in an elementary school. It was a writing assignment where 3 to 4 paragraphs were needed to complete the essay.

Colby lumbered up to my desk with a friendly smile and uttered, "Mr. A, I finished all the questions and have written four paragraphs!"

He dutifully handed me his paper, and I noticed right away that even though he was the first one to finish, I could hardly make out a word because his letters were so sloppy.

I looked at him and said, "it looks like you were trying to get this done quickly, am I right?" "Yes Mr. A, I usually beat everybody in the class, and have my work done first!" he exclaimed with enthusiasm.

"Well that would be great if this was a race, but all this is just a writing assignment that your teacher Mrs. Stearns will be grading, that is if she can read this. Do you think Colby that someone else can decipher this handwriting?"

"Of course they could read my writing can't you?" Colby looked at me with a condescending look and snide attitude about him.

"As a matter of fact young man I can only make out a few words."

As he returned to his seat he begrudgingly stared at his paper, and began to write much more slowly and pensively. He returned quite a bit later with a much better product.

He told me later when I subbed at that school that he didn't want to do the work over, but it was that encounter with me that helped him see that in the long run he needed to skip the scribble dibble, and adopt a much neater way of writing.

Subbing affords us the opportunity to not just keep order in a classroom, and do what the teacher wants, but also to impart something that can improve the student's academic life.

In 2010 the U.S. government officially removed cursive from the common core standards. More recently California, who is no stranger to taking new initiatives, signed into law on October 17th 2023 that it is mandatory for students to learn cursive.

Regardless of which side of that fence you are on, there are pluses and minuses with each camp.

People that favor doing just manuscript say that time could be better spent on keyboards.

People who favor teaching cursive say that writing it helps one express themselves, and that a lot of neurodiverse and disabled kids do better with cursive.

So you ask what does this have to do with substitute teaching?

Good question!

As a sub I found that I can plant good seeds in students' hearts.

Especially when I sub in elementary schools, I try to show them the benefit of writing neatly whether it be manuscript/printing or cursive/writing.

I like to demonstrate on the board my scribble dibble when I was younger. Usually this gets some chuckles and heightens the attention of my students.

Then I show them by writing on the board how going slower can make my letters much neater. I admit to them, "When I was young and not interested in much about school, I went so fast just trying to get my work done so I could go play.

I say to them, "let me tell you a secret about your teachers. None of them like sloppy writing. It takes longer to read so it wastes their time, plus the teacher knows you can do much better."

When I was a kid, if you would have asked me if I wanted to be rich or poor I would have said rich with a smile on my face."

Then I make the parallel between scribbling and laziness. Lazy people just scribble because it takes more effort to write neatly, but when one puts the right effort into their work, I show them that hard work is the only way to go.

scribble= lazy= poor
neat writing= hard work= $

SUMMARY:
1- Neatness in writing should be emphasized.
2- Encourage students, (especially the boys), LOL, to slow down to make their letters more legible.

9- NESTING OR NON NESTING? WHICH IS RIGHT FOR YOU?

The days of waiting for a phone call to get a sub job are rare!

Now the vast majority of school districts rely on a computer automated system that alerts subs as to the potential jobs that are available.

Over the course of subbing for well over a decade I have discerned two types of subbing styles:

NESTERS- Substitute Teachers that go to the same location every day and the school puts them wherever is needed. The obvious benefit here is they are going to the same location every day, and do not have to go through the process of finding jobs off the web. A drawback can be that the school might ask you to go above and beyond what a normal sub does because of over familiarity. I did this with an elementary school for half a school year and really enjoyed it.

Why?

Mostly because the school system I was subbing at really had it together. The teachers loved working there, and the school maintained good student academics and discipline. They also respected my position, and did not ask me to do a bunch of extra duties.

NON-NESTERS- Substitute Teachers nowadays use the web to pick the jobs that they are the most comfortable with. I have always been the most comfortable with high school. You may have a different age group preference. Maybe you enjoy the younger students? As you sub this will come to light.

One note of caution when you are trying to get jobs off the web. I have noticed that sometimes there is not enough definition on the description. For instance it may say, "floater," for an elementary school and your comfort zone in elementary schools is working in 4-6 grade, then you get to this elementary school and the job is kindergarten or following an autistic child all day.

And you say to yourself, "this is not what I had in mind."

You get the picture.

"No Fly List"- Some teachers and some schools earned this designation in my phone book where I keep my records. What do I mean by "No Fly List"? Very simply said it means that the experience I had in a particular classroom or even the whole school did not merit a return visit.

I have had a few, "One and Done," schools over the years. Last year I went to a middle school that earned the nefarious and dubious label of permanent, "No Fly List."

Why?

If I am in a class where there are a few students that need correction no problem, but in this particular school there was a culture of disrespect. Disruption was not the exception; it was the rule. One and Done!

Another big problem with this school was when I called for an administrator to come and take the unruly students away, it was 25-30 minutes before they showed up.

Also you may have a situation where you like the school, and want to continue, but you have an assignment whereas as soon as you open the door to the room, you have this bad feeling that it is going to be a long day. The room is a big mess, the lesson plans are nebulous and hard to read, or there were no plans there at all. The students have not been trained to be quiet, when quiet is the expectation of you in the lesson plans, and the day just drags on, because you are on a train that has been allowed to get off the tracks often.

This teacher is awarded the, "No Fly," designation.

I have learned that good organization and administration saves time.

SUMMARY:

1- Finding your "comfort zone in subbing," and what age group you work best with is the key to wanting to return back to work each day.

10- DOCUMENTATION

Recently I ended up in the high school hood. The school I went to has a graduating class of 350 to 400 kids, and just a few classes were easy to sub in. Many of these high school students needed to learn and practice good behavior.

However on this particular day I ended up with kids that didn't want to sit down and weren't going to stop talking. They were disrespectful and very disruptive.

That can be an easy recipe for me to get on the phone and call an administrator and they come and scoop up a few disorderly students to bring to the office, and it can also be a sure formula to calm the rest of the calamitous natives down.

Taking attendance is always a challenge with an unruly squad like this bunch. Just pronouncing names can be a tongue twisting enigma. Then when you don't say it just right, the inappropriate outburst of the offended student, who in reality is just putting on a feigned display of displeasure just to draw the sub off. This can really get me out of my rhythm in doing the roll. Remember this is usually limited to high school misbehavior.

I get it that this generation of parents want their children's names to be unique, but those same parents can easily forget that they are parents and not their kid's buddy. Thus the end product is kids that are disrespectful, distractors, and over all obstinate.

With every class I ever sub in, I do a cover sheet to give a report to the teacher about each class. If the teacher is organized, which thankfully, is usually the case, then I thank and compliment them in writing for this.

The cover sheet then extends to a summary of the class's overall behavior and performance.

The other place the regular teacher can get information is on the handwritten rooming chart that I construct. Disruptive students I move to another desk, this is known as redirecting. Children that won't stop talking, and students that do nothing, or sleep, will get a note about them on this chart.

I also write down my phone number if the regular teacher has any questions they can text or call me. Also if I liked the classes, I will encourage the teacher to contact me if I could serve them in the future.

Documenting as much as possible becomes a two pronged advantage over the sub that does not practice this helpful discipline:

1- It is so useful to inform the regular teacher of the day's happenings. How did the students work, did they get along, were they attentive? respectful? etc.

2- I can take a picture of my documentation for my own records.

Writing things down just makes sense. Time goes by quickly and trying to recall events can be difficult. Remember, "the weakest pen is stronger than the strongest memory."

SUMMARY:

1- One of the most important functions you do is take attendance so develop a system where you write things down and are thorough and work for you.

11- WHY IS SUBBING A GOOD CHOICE

"Hey boss, I see you are at the bottom of the barrel!" Clyde looked over at Mr. A ,and had a good ole chuckle and displayed his chewing tobacco stained teeth and missing a tooth smile.

"OK good buddy, by the way, are you referring to my present place of employment?"

The two pals were playing some 8 ball at the local sports bar. Clyde was kicking Mr. A's butt and had won 3 games in a row.

"Yeah man, how long have you been subbing anyway?"

Clyde took a long drag on his filterless cigarette. He loved to blow the smoke so that the circles that came out of his mouth were perfectly spaced.

"Well to tell ya the truth, I'm actually at the top of the pecking order!" Mr. A gave his friend a warm smile.

"You are full of bologna!" Clyde who loved to ridicule his Yankee pal retorted with a gleeful gaze.

The two men were two peas but not from the same pod. Clyde was a good old boy with a beer belly who loved to laugh and tease his Northern pal who by the way just loved his Bronx Bombers and everything about the "Big Apple," as Mr. A had been raised in Upstate New York.

Mr. A then proceeded to give Clyde the one two punch why his job was the head and not the tail.

"For starters I tell them when I want to work. Then there is the fact that I have no lesson plans to slave over, no parents to deal with, and when the day's work is done, I don't have the ongoing weight of the job on my shoulders when I go home. That's why I ended up with the best job in the place, amigo, wouldn't you agree?"

Clyde nodded and with a twinkle in his eye said, "well dog gone it, you're not as stupid as I thought you were!"

That was as close to a compliment as Mr. A thought he had ever heard coming out of his buddy's lips, and he just laughed to himself.

The plain fact is that most retired seniors in the United States have sources of income that others do not, therefore most of them really do not have to work but many choose to.

There are some that still need to work and substitute teaching is a great way to do it.

Concerning college students there are many who want to go into education, but before they go through four years of college, and have to pay for all that, wouldn't it be a good idea for many of them to substitute teach? This way they can experience what the water is really like in the world of teaching.

It's really easy to get a job. Substitute teacher agencies such as Kelly and ESS make it pretty simple to sign up and start doing the job.

So yes, college students who are thinking about becoming teachers, this can be a wonderful way for them to see if in fact they like being in the classroom in that role.

Virtually anyone could go down this road of being a substitute teacher. The only requirements are: checking out your police record via fingerprinting, and all agencies require a drug test.

SUMMARY:
1- Substitute teaching is a job that anyone 21 and over can tackle.

12- ADMINISTRATORS: TO CALL OR NOT TO CALL

"Would you please be seated, Ann?"

After I said that a second time, she stared at me with obvious disdain and very slowly sat down.

"Noah, are you here? After two tries, I usually go on to the next one on the roster. Turns out he was here but the class was so loud, he said later he never heard me.

"OK class your assignment is on the board," at this point I still only have about half the class's attention. I use the pause and stare technique, but to no avail. I'm thinking this is going to be a long class.

So now I change strategies and raise the volume of my voice.

At this just 3 or 4 of the twenty some odd students remain talking and showing blatant disrespect.

I put a mark by where they are seated as I do not have their names yet, I'm still taking roll.

As I am nearing the end of taking attendance. Noah decides to start, "milling," around the classroom.

Milling is a word I use to describe one of a few no-nos in my classroom. It is when a student is walking around with no purpose, usually with the intent of drawing attention to themselves.

All the students know they should not be doing this, but today the class has a sub and you guessed it some of the established boundaries will be tested.

At this point I call Noah over to my desk, and as he is very slowly making his way over for the unwanted, "chat," with the silver haired sub, I can see his face is starting to lose the smirk on it.

"Is there some reason you are slowly just walking around the room, it seems like you are not going anywhere in particular Mr. Noah?"

"I need to sharpen my pencil." He then notices that I am pointing to his hands.

"Well, where is the pencil?"

At this I get a blank stare.

The classroom is hushed by now waiting to hear how this misbehavior is being corrected by the sub. The only problem is they can't hear what we're saying, because I'm making sure we whisper and are having a private conversation.

I have found that this is a great technique for reproof because you're not embarrassing the student in front of their peers, and trying to have an honest conversation about what is going on…it can be very effective. Unfortunately, not always, because some students do choose not to change or don't tell the truth.

The conversation with Noah ended with him going back to his desk, and actually doing his work for the rest of that class.

I was glad that all he needed was to be redirected.

Meanwhile the commotion is continuing on the other side of the classroom. Isn't it interesting that the students who are the farthest away from the teacher have a tendency to try to get away with more. Have you ever noticed that?

Ben and Anna's desks had somehow gotten right next to each other. Also I noticed that their legs were touching each others and their hands were on the other's body.

As I was standing at the front of the class, I got their attention and asked them softly to put their desks back to where they were originally, like everybody else.

Ben looked at me with disgust and barked, "Ms. Johnston, let's study together!" As if to say to me, who the heck are you to tell us what to do?

I calmly replied, "Please put your desks back in the way they were aligned at the beginning of class."

At this the other offender chimed in, "We don't have to do what you say, you are just a lousy sub!"

At this I begin to slowly walk toward the phone and then I stop and turn back at the two of them. Do you both really want to leave the room right now? You are both not following directions and you're becoming a disturbance and disruption in the classroom.

Both of them refused to look at me when I was talking to them, and did not respond. So I felt I had no other recourse than to call the administration and have them removed.

Meanwhile other students were continuing to talk loudly and be disruptive.

When the administrator arrived I thanked her for coming and apologized for having to bother her.

I said out loud and in a big voice these students are not following directions and are being disruptive. Would you please take them out of the classroom?

Then I turned to the class and said briskly and loud enough so all could hear, and by the way at this point in time you could see all were quiet in the classroom, "is there anyone else that needs to leave?"

No response.

"I'm just checking because I don't want to have to bother this administrator or anyone else at the office, but you all need to know that I document everything that happens in the classroom, especially things that are of a derogatory or negative nature like this."

The rest of the class was smooth sailing.

One of the reasons why the schools like me so well as a sub is I rarely have to call administration, because I try to handle all the difficult students within the classroom, but then when it gets to the point where unless I really get on the phone, those students will take over the behavior of the classroom, and that I cannot allow, neither should you.

Here are some tips I use to truly try and fend off the last resort of turning to the phone and removing the student:

1- The appeal: when a student is getting verbally disruptive and too loud for the class, I usually call them over to the desk after attendance and make an appeal to them to stop that behavior. I let them know that I have put a check mark by their name on the chart, which will mean nothing if that's all there is when the teacher gets the report tomorrow, but if they continue that behavior then I'll either have to remove them or just write them up.

2- The relocation: sometimes all that's needed is to move a student that's being disruptive to another part of the classroom and that puts out the fire.

3- The helpful teacher next door: many times when I'm subbing in elementary schools the teacher next door knows who the problem children are, and they will say to me, "if you need to send anybody over to me just go right ahead." This is a big help! I've had to do this on various occasions.

4- Give the whole class my patented speech: this usually goes something like this, "I really enjoy substitute teaching and like all my students. Until such time as they decide to misbehave."

I'm just hoping that this class decides to take the high road of doing your work, and not being disruptors. Is there anybody here who can raise their hand, and tell us what the word disruption means?" Then I turn that into a teaching moment.

5- Use the phone as the neutral object for correction: especially in Senior High School everyone knows that the only real teeth that a substitute teacher has in trying to control an unruly classroom is the phone. Just like the wise parent, who spanks their child when they're disobedient, but they've learned not to use their hand but a neutral object like a wooden spoon or a small flat board.

This is so the child will not fear a person's body, but rather the neutral object. My wife and I, raising two daughters, used a wooden spoon and after effectively practicing, "the rod," all my wife had to do was look like she was reaching for the drawer where the spoon was located, and the bad attitude or the lousy voice would change immediately.

You can see where I'm going with this, trying to turn this into a discussion where the students realize that:

A. Disruptive behavior will not be tolerated.

B. A class full of goof offs will also not be tolerated, especially in elementary school, sometimes I make exceptions on this one depending on whether I'm in high school, because when they get that old and they just don't want to work it's like the old saying, "you can lead a horse to water but you can't make them drink."

C. Standing or walking around the room is not allowed.

So then as a sub when should I call administration?

To call or not to call that is the question…

I need to be honest with you. My tendency is to labor too long with children that should have been sent out a while back.

I believe this is something that you have to gauge by how students are actually following the rules, coupled with the kind of attitude they display, while they interact with you about those rules.

SUMMARY:
1- Only call an administrator as the last resort to keep order in the class. Make a serious effort to retain every student to stay in your classroom.

13- WHICH HAT TO WEAR? VERSATILITY A NECESSITY

"So did you really want me to put on my military hat and be a sergeant or would you prefer a nice, quiet, calm substitute teacher?" I was looking at two students in the back who were way over the top in bad behavior.

"Alright Mr. A we hear ya!" With that the two young men decided to stop the loud and boisterous behavior.

Substitute teaching just like any position and job dealing with people should involve a great deal of versatility.

John Rockefeller who at one point in history was the richest man and owner of Standard Oil, who retired in his fifties, said this concerning people.

"I will pay more for this one thing than anything: the ability to work with people."

Why did he say this?

I believe he did because he knew that people had various types of different needs, and sundry personalities and a broad array of struggles, and it takes a great deal of wisdom to know how to deal with all these types of people.

Thus the need to have different hats,(strategies), to be able to meet the various needs of different people.

One wise man by the name of Paul said this, "I have become all things to all men that I might by all means…" that sounds like versatility to me, and the more that we can practice this in our dealings with people, the more effective I believe we will be.

One sure fire practice that I put on every day when I go to work as a substitute teacher is the one that says kindness and I care about you.

Students seem to always be in great need of love. I believe once students truly realize that a teacher deeply cares for them, and wants what's best for them, then that attribute more than any other, becomes the highway by which the student can receive instruction, and grow into a responsible adult, and a citizen who is productive for society.

SUMMARY:
1- Be ready to be all things to all students. By becoming what you sense, they need.

14- SUBBING IN ELEMENTARY, MIDDLE AND HIGH SCHOOL.

"Hey Carol, when are you going to get your masters degree in elementary education?" Susan was putting the Splenda in her coffee in the teachers lounge, and just saw her friend walk into the room.

"I'm going to try and get it all done online via the University of Phoenix. I've also looked into Liberty University. Both programs are within my budget, and I think very doable.

"Well girl, if I was you, I'd get the lead out, our dear principal has a timetable when it comes to these things, and you're going to want to let him know you're on the fast track to get your master's degree. Susan was starting to sip her coffee but realized it was way too hot still.

"All right there Miss Drill Sergeant I've got it on the radar and want to get it done ASAP." Carol was starting to feel like her friend was getting pushy.

"So what exactly do you like about teaching kindergarten anyways?"

"Well for starters they just don't talk back, in fact some of them hardly talk at all!" Carol let out a bit of a guarded laugh at this comment. She continued, "I also love the innocence that I see in this age group, and frankly they really just want to learn without all the other fluff, and baggage that the older age groups seem to have."

"I can see that. So is there any downside?" Susan concurred.

"Not really, hey when you sincerely love something, it's like you are not working, that's how I feel about teaching kindergarten full time."

Some people like Carol just love it. I on the other hand do not and avoid the early age groups.

Why? It's a lot of work plus the real young ones are still learning what, " no," means.

Why? Too much work to do, and I do not have a love for that age group.

Little Emma and Jose have not learned what the word, "No," means yet.

" Mr. A tie my shoe, Mr. A Help me blow my nose, Mr. A, I think I had an accident, Mr. A, when do I get to go home? Mr. A, is it snack time? Mr. A, I can't find my knapsack!" Can you see the need for the patience of Job?

Some folks love this age group. I admire them and their perseverance and hard work ethic.

This group is just not my cup of tea. So I must pass on offering much advice except that you really know you love this age group before you sign up for it.

Third through fifth grade I have found to be a great fit, as long as the school has developed a culture where the students have learned respect, and how to work on their own, quietly.

They are at an age where they can learn and assimilate information rapidly. I call it the, "wet cement stage." I really enjoy teaching this group. They are so impressionable, and it's a privilege to impact them with great information, and the importance of good character

Middle School is a different animal altogether. I refer to this group as, "attitude on steroids." Puberty and preteen can be a dangerous combo, and this bunch can be very challenging, but highly rewarding if you are up to it.

High School to me is the easiest gig for subbing that there is. I liken this to being similar to the uncle watching the kids for the parents. Will the kids try to get away with more not being watched by the parents,...of course!

After attendance, they will either do their work or not, regardless of what you do or don't do.

Translation, because they are bigger they require little or no maintenance. Thus more time for me to get paid, while I read a book or write a book like this!

Basically you do three things:

1- take attendance, (do a handwritten rooming chart).

2- Write the assignment on the board. Usually placing,"Google Classroom," on the board is sufficient.

3- Make sure students stay seated unless they are going to the restroom or some other legitimate place in the classroom to get something. Use a rooming chart to keep track of time they are gone to the restroom. One time I had a student leave for 27 minutes. It will be up to the teacher to reprove the student when they return.

A side note, it never fails, when a class first comes in, many students will ask to go to the restroom then. I simply say, "not till after attendance."

Many schools have a 10 minute rule. This means the first 10 minutes of class and 10 minutes before class ends you may not go to the restroom.

Inevitably students will ask me if they can go to the library or some other location. My simple and honest response is this, "I am only authorized to send you to one place, the bathroom, that is the school policy."

So get ready to be unpopular as the, "substitute order keeper."

SUMMARY:
1- Subbing at the different age groups usually takes a different set of skills.

15- CELL PHONES: THE ELEPHANT IN THE ROOM?

"But my teacher lets me,"study," with my cell phone!"

"We are allowed to use our smartphones in class!"

These are the pleas that the students, especially high schoolers tell the, "Uncle," watching the class.

That "Uncle," is me the sub!

I found out real quick that I had about as much authority in some schools as a gnat in a swamp full of hippos!

When I arrived at the school to get my marching orders for the day, the bookkeeper smiled and handed me a few papers clipped together.

The 8 ½ x 11 on top had 7 bullet type sentences which were the DON'TS for substitute teachers.

The 5th rule was NO CELL PHONES ALLOWED IN CLASS!

This would be all well and good but there was one big problem!

The regular teachers, I would find out, or at least a lot of them succumbed to the pressure of the students to use their beloved smartphones in the classroom.

The depersonalization due to smartphone infiltration into society caused Chick fil A to offer families free ice cream, if they would just turn in their cell phones at the counter and actually talk to one another!

There were a few times I tried to enforce this rule that the teachers themselves weren't, and I was met with tantrums and overt misbehavior.

Sad to say our schools are being taken over by Google, Apple, Corporate AI, and the cyber instructors, who don't give a hoot about the character development of a student.

Thus the easy choice of teachers to let the students not learn to think for themselves, put on the headphones and let the laptop take over or worse the smartphone seems all to ever-present.

The Elephant in the Room?

Could it be that the smartphone itself is a part of what George Orwell's book, "1984," foresaw? Having learned how to get in the classroom and addict the student to listen and watch the enticing empty video platitudes that lead to a shallow and lazy American adult, it all begs the question will the U.S.A. have any leaders in the future that will honestly be fit enough to take our country successfully into the years ahead?

SUMMARY:
1- Cell phones are usually a detriment in any classroom and can become a major league distraction.

16- HOW TO OVERCOME FEAR

"We got a sub!" The mischievous twinkle in the eyes of the two boys with jerseys on as they strutted into class was written all over their faces."

Other students joined that chorus of, "Hooray a sub!"

Ploys of how to embarass, harass, and plots to take over the class by misbehavior were forming in the minds of these rascals in the Earth Science class.

Attendance was longer than usual because the students were slow to identify themselves when called on. Loud conversations, many were giggling, and screwing around, it was really looking like a wayward class.

Finally I realized it was time to pull the plug on all the talking, and if need be challenge the ringleaders of the forced commotion, and over the top disruption, to cease and desist or I would most likely need to get on the phone, and have certain disruptors removed.

"Alright, no more talking in class, I'm having serious problems taking attendance."

This halted the talking.

As I continued to take role the two boys with the jerseys on kept up with the loud chatter, and laughter trying to draw others into the fray they were creating.

At this I began to walk toward the phone, and then stopped, turned and looked back at them and said, "Do you really want me to call the administrator and have you removed?"

At this one of the boys said, "No Sir." I then stared at the other one for his response.

His delay was way too long. He was clearly wasting time.

I made the call. He was taken away, probably to I.S.S. (In School Suspension), the other boy who answered respectfully was allowed to stay.

I have been in many similar situations, I always try to find the leaders of the misbehavior, which is not always the easiest thing to do.

They must be confronted firmly and given a chance to change.

A lot of the disruptors are looking for fear in you, or at the very least to get you agitated.

How does one overcome fear?

1- Realize and affirm to yourself that you are the adult in the room.
2- Look everyone in the eye.
3- Use a voice where the students discover who is really in charge...YOU!
4- Warnings should be direct and given with an air of certainty. "I need you to sit over here now, the next relocation will be out of the room."

I'm going to need it completely quiet now."

"Did you really want me to write you up?"

You can put the ball in their court with a question, and this way many students turn away from the foolish behavior they are exhibiting.

There are many ways you can firmly confront, yet we are always hoping for the students to make better choices, and not face expulsion from the class.

5- If you are a person of faith, agree with Paul when he says, "God has not given me a spirit of fear, but of power, love and a sound mind."

Summary:
1- Fear can cripple you from being effective as a substitute teacher. Face your fears with overcoming faith.

17- IDEAS

A- Make a hand written rooming list. Take your time and do this for attendance especially with the elementary grades, make eye contact with each student when you call their name, and you can also use that as a quick check on the students attitude on how they respond.

B- Find out the names of school disciplinarians- sometimes just mentioning the name of the principal or the disciplinarians that come to the room, if there's a problem, can be enough to stop wrong behavior.

C- Have the administration phone number handy, (some schools have a button you push when there's a problem), if you do need to call for help having the number handy is essential.

D- Discern the protocol of each individual classroom as soon as you can. Does the regular teacher allow talking? How are bathroom requests handled? etc.

E- Once you arrive in the classroom make sure that the rooming roster for attendance is there, and there are lesson plans. Many times if either is missing just a quick call to the office will take care of it. I write the lesson plan for the students on the board, this way I do not have to keep repeating myself. Make sure you have the sheet with the times that they switch classes.

F- Introduce yourself to the teacher next door and ask if there is anything that you should know.

APPENDIX

Please direct all correspondence to:

davidballport@gmail.com

The author is available to answer your questions, and would be glad to assist and help you in any way.

Made in the USA
Columbia, SC
14 November 2024

46397218R00054